D1715800

BYRON KATIE

on

Work and Money

Edited by Stephen Mitchell

the work of
byron katie
WWW.THEWORK.COM

BYRON KATIE INTERNATIONAL, INC. • LOS ANGELES

Published in the United States by:
Byron Katie International, Inc.
578 Washington Blvd. Box 821
Marina del Rey, CA 90292
1 800-98KATIE (52843)
www.thework.com

ISBN 1-890246-80-8

Printed in the United States of America.
Design & Layout by Balsam Design
Art Director: Richard Balsam
Production Specialist: Emily Eoff
Cover Photography: Brie Childers

To Josh Baran,
with love and gratitude

The Work of Byron Katie:
The Four Questions and Turnaround

1. Is it true?
2. Can you absolutely know that it's true?
3. How do you react when you believe that thought?
4. Who would you be without the thought?
   and

Turn it around.

For some of us, life is controlled by our thoughts about work and money. But if our thinking is clear, how could work or money be the problem? Our thinking is all we need to change. It's all we *can* change. This is very good news.

This Work is about doing business with clarity and vision, without any fear.

What you want money for is to buy you happiness. This Work will give you happiness without money. And it becomes very clear that money is not that important. So you become unattached to money, and then it can't help but find you. That's a law.

Some people believe that fear and stress are what motivate them to make money. But can you really know that that's true? Can you be absolutely certain that without fear or stress as a motivator, you wouldn't have made the same money, or even more? "I need stress to motivate me"—who would you be if you never believed that story again?

The job you do out there in the apparent world is secondary. It's only a place for you to judge, inquire, and know yourself. Your true job is to appreciate what is; your primary profession is to be clear.

A material thing is a symbol of your thinking. It's a metaphor. We don't have to give up our things. They come or go; we have no control over that. We may think we do, but in reality we don't. Whoever started teaching that we need to let go of things, to detach from them, was a little confused. We notice that if we lose everything we're much freer, so we think that it's better to live impoverished. And then we notice that we're not free anymore. Everything changes. But when we work with our thinking, then to have great wealth is the same as to have nothing. That's the only freedom.

We think that because Gandhi wore a loincloth, and Jesus wore robes, that's how it's supposed to look. But can you have a normal life and be free? Can you do it from where you are? Can you do it from here now? When you're lying on your feather bed, can you be free there? That's what I want. We have the same desire: your freedom. And I love that you're attached to material objects, so that you can come to know your own freedom, whether you have them or not.

Money is not my business, my thinking is my business. I don't have any other business.

You think that your life would be much better with that green car because having that car means something. What is it? It could just mean that you have a green car. You drive down the street and somebody thinks, "Oh my god, what is she doing with a green car?" Somebody else says, "Wow! She's got a green car!" Somebody else says, "Hmpf! How come she gets to have a green car?" It means whatever you think it means.

We don't attach to things, we attach to our stories about them. I don't hold on to my car, I hold on to the story about my car. It's beautiful, it's old, it's falling apart, it's in great running condition, I need it to go to work, I would be in trouble if I didn't have it, it's cool, it makes me look good, it lets people know that I'm doing well—that's what we're attached to. Without the story, no car. I don't mean we would or wouldn't physically have a car. Instead, it would be "woman getting into car going to work" or "woman losing her job with something better coming along, and getting onto bus to go to work."

For people who enter this inner world, the world of inquiry, jobs become secondary. Freedom is everything. Jobs come, jobs go, companies rise and fall, and you're not dependent on that. Freedom is what we all want, and it's what we already are. And once

you have inquiry, you can be as ambitious as
you want in your job, you can shoot for the
moon, because you can no longer fail. You
realize that the worst that can happen
is a concept.

The heart can sing, can't it! That's what you
wanted money for. Well, you can skip that
part, and just sing. It doesn't mean you won't
have money too. Can you do it for richer
or poorer, as the world sees it? Yes, and all
you've done is begin to tap into you—that's

all that has happened. You've just answered
a few questions from deep inside you. Who
would you be if you never believed the story
"I need money" again? You've believed that
if you didn't think you needed money, you
would never have it. But the truth is that
having money never had anything to do
with thinking you needed it or not. There's
nothing to know here. You don't have to know
anything. There's ultimately nothing you can
do to make money or to stop making money.

The Work is about internal cause and effect. It's not about external things.

After I found The Work inside myself—after it found me—I began to notice that I always had the perfect amount of money for me right now, even when I had little or none. Happiness is a clear mind. A clear and sane mind knows how to live, how to work, what e-mails to send, what phone calls to make, and what to do to create what it wants without fear. Do you want your money to be safe and secure? Hopeless! Read my lips: hopeless! Banks burn, countries are bombed, people lie, they break their promises, they bend contracts. It's hopeless, hopeless. How do you live when you believe the thought that your money should be safe? Who would you be without the thought "I need my money to be safe"? You might be a lot easier to be with. You might even begin to notice the laws of generosity, the laws of letting money go out fearlessly and come back fearlessly. You don't ever need more money than you have. When you understand this, you begin to realize that you already have all the security you wanted money to give you in the first place. It's a lot easier to make money from this position. The money comes because it's with the appropriate keeper. This concept "I want my money to be safe" puts you in the position of the miser. So it goes out miserly, it comes back miserly. And even if it comes back in the billions, it still doesn't feel that way, because you've attached to the concept "I have to make it safe." So you're not the keeper of it, you're afflicted with it. *It*'s keeping *you*. When you live the turnaround—"I want my *thinking* to be safe"—you don't need money. You have all the security you wanted money to give you in the first place. Money is like air—it's everywhere. There's nothing you can do not to have it. And if you don't have it, it's because you don't need it. So you can skip the money part and be free! You don't ever need more money than you have. When you understand this, you begin to realize that you already have all the security you wanted money to give you in the first place. It's a lot easier to make money from this position.

"You have to work" has never been true, it's
the lie you hold on to so that you can keep
yourself from the joy of the gift that you give.
No one has to work. No one has ever had to.

"Your money shouldn't go to other people
without your permission"—is that true?
That's a wonderful myth. And what's the
reality of it? *Does* your money go to other
people without your permission? Of course it
does. So the statement is a lie. Because you're
a miser with your money, sometimes, you

think you have control over where it goes. But all you're doing is proving to yourself that this lie works, the lie that you have control, so you try to get tighter control. It's a godless place. It leaves you alone, with no connection. And that's terrifying, and really lonely. In that space, when you have money, you attribute that to your miserliness. So you're teaching yourself that you have the money because you're a miser, and it's an illusion. You have it because you have it. You're not in control. A tree puts out leaves without your help. A baby is born, and you didn't even know. This is abundance. You did nothing to get it.

Wealth and poverty are in your own mind.
You could be rich with ten dollars, or poor
with a billion dollars. It's just your story about
money that strikes terror in your heart. Has
there ever been a time in your life when you
didn't have enough? There's abundance all
around you, and you don't even notice. Not
only do you have clothes, but you have clothes
under them; not only do you have ears, but
you have earrings. Who would you be without
the thought that you don't have enough?
Who would you be without this belief that
you think will scare you into making money?
Even though you don't believe in slavery, you

are the slave and the slave owner. And it
wears you out brutally, until you don't
even want to go to work.

Go to the top of your Worksheet and read
everything you wrote, substituting the word
mother for *money*. Are you beginning to see
how we only attach to beliefs, that there's no
such thing as money or mother or any of it?
The concept is our god. We investigate the
concept, and we lose the whole world, which
never existed in the first place. It's not the

money or the mother that is the problem. It is the concept you're attached to.

You haven't been taking care of yourself, you've been taking care of your money. "I'll take care of myself after I have enough money, after I get it secured. I'll be happy then." And "then" never comes.

"Money is exciting and adventurous"—is that true? It just sits there! It's even boring—all those little faces. Money does nothing—it just sits there. It doesn't think, it doesn't feel, it doesn't know, it doesn't care, it doesn't show favorites, it just is. A piece of metal. A piece of paper. Even gold bullion is just that. The story you put onto it is what thrills you, what interests you, what scares you. You tell the story of what money is doing, what it's going to do, how it should come and go, and you heaven or hell you. But money just sits there. Without a story, it's just not personal. You get to the place where you don't care if you live or die because you're having so much fun investigating these concepts. And someone tells you, "You don't have any money," and you say "Oh! I didn't know that." Or they ask, "How come you have millions of dollars?" and you say, "I do?" The internal world is so fine. There's nothing that can compete with it.

It doesn't matter what symbol we use. The master is the one in front of you. So if money is your symbol, good. We all have our symbols. And if you accumulate more money

than you could ever spend, you'll just find a
different symbol.

You are your own boss. Even if you have the
most menial job in the world, you are your
boss. And if you don't like your job, welcome
to The Work.

Can you really know that your highest good
is to be an artist? How do you react when you

believe that thought? You refuse to be content in a job less lofty than that, and when you get a job you hate it because you think you're just marking time until you can devote yourself to your art. So you're always living in the future, and you're never present. Who would you be without your story that you're supposed to have a career as an artist? You'd be that saint down there flipping burgers or scrubbing floors. You'd be in my favorite position: the position of servant.

Poverty is internal. Every time that you think you know something you're experiencing poverty.

"You're supposed to be seen at work, for who you are"—is that true? Did you put it in your job description? Does your contract say "If you do this and this and this, then we will see you"? Put that in the contract before you take the job, tell the boss, "Yes, I see the requirements here, and I have one of my own: I need to be seen at work." You go to work and you think we should see you, and we are just doing our job here, people pay us, we've made a commitment, but according to you we should take time out to see our legal secretary, she needs to be seen. That's what you're asking, you're asking us to drop our integrity, so that you can be seen. When you think we should see you and we don't, you disconnect, and what does that have to do with us? How do you react when you believe this insane thought that you need to be seen? You get to go blank, you get to hate your job and call it us. Who would you be if you didn't believe the thought that we should stop what we're doing and see you? You might be someone who didn't stop to see if we were seeing you. You might be someone who stayed in her own business. And you might be someone who loves her job. You would see your job instead of this theory that we should see you. And then when you got your paycheck, you would love it, because you would know that you had earned it and you hadn't cheated. No job has ever bothered you, only your thinking has bothered you. You only have one job: to come into alignment with your thinking. And the way you do that is that you write it down, then

apply four questions and a turnaround, and
go inside for your answers.

The future shows me why the money comes in.
It's backward. I'm a conduit. There's nothing I
can do not to have everything I need.

If you don't know what the truth is, it will
be there for you. It's called reality. Reality—

that's the last place we look. How does it feel when you have one job, and you think you should be doing something else? It's very painful. Who would you be without the story "I should be doing something different"? Doing what you do, present, efficient, available. And when you are that clear as an employee, you don't last long in that position, they promote you. It's called integrity. It's a well that's bottomless, it's so vast. "I should be doing something different"—turn it around. "I should not be doing something different." Not now. Maybe it will change, but right now this job is good. The only thing that's not good about now is a story that would keep you from it.

Many of us are motivated by a desire for success. But what is success? What do we want to achieve? We do only three things in life: we stand, we sit, we lie horizontal. Once we've found success, we'll still be sitting somewhere, until we stand, and we'll stand until we lie down or sit again. Success is a concept, an illusion. Do you want the $3900 chair instead of the $39 one? Well, sitting is sitting. And for the word *chair* you could substitute *car* or *house* or *business*. You can only sit in one place at one time. If I think that I should have a different chair, just to use that metaphor, I am insane! I am wanting two things at once, and confusion is the only suffering. "I want another chair," is a lie. What I want is this chair, obviously, because that's the one I'm sitting in. So I'm no longer confused. How do I know I want this chair? I'm sitting in it.

The truth is that the job that you hate—you really love it. Except for your beliefs, it's the job for you. How do I know? It's the one you have! You can own the company you're working for if you just realized that you're not there because you have to be at that job. Drop all your beliefs around it, and we want you, we'll pay you anything, you're irresistible, you're love in action.

The thought "I have to go to work" makes your life a war zone. Whereas if you just wake up

knowing to go to work, you just go, you just go
in peace, and work is a pleasure. But when you
argue with reality, the beliefs pile up, and the
office becomes a sweatshop.

When should you fire someone? That's simple:
when you want the job done. Do you want the
job done or not? Just stop fooling yourself.
This way you can talk to that person from
an understanding position, because you are
being responsible for your own life. I once
did The Work with an executive who said, "My

assistant has been with me for ten years. I know she doesn't do the job well, but she has five children." I said, "Good. Keep her here so she can teach the rest of your employees that if they have enough children, they can work for you, whether they do their job well or not." And he said, "Well, I just can't fire her." I said, "I understand that. So put someone qualified in her position, send her home to her five children who need her, and send her a paycheck every month. That's more honest than what you're doing now. Guilt is expensive." When the executive read his Worksheet to the woman, she agreed with every single thing he had written about her job performance, because it was clear and true. And I said to her, "What do you suggest? What would you do if you were *your* employee?" People usually fire themselves when they realize what's going on, and that's just what she did. She found a similar job in another company, closer to her home, where she was able to be both a good assistant and a good mother. The executive realized that he had never investigated the thoughts that led him to be "loyal" to an assistant who, in reality, had been just as uncomfortable with the situation as he was.

Your job is not about making money, or working with people, or impressing your friends, or getting respect. The job is about your freedom. Everything—every man, woman, and child, every tree, every stone—is about your freedom. It's all God giving you what you need so you can get honest one time.

If everyone knew to do the Work, there would be no unemployment. How could there be any unemployment, since there is only one job: to know yourself?

Your fears are nothing more than a lack of integrity, that's all, there's no mystery. Write them down, inquire, and notice how they just don't arise any more, and if they do, they have encountered a friend, and there's peace. Fear is lack of integrity, and the way that you know that is that when you're in a lie, you experience discomfort. Life is simple, until you lose your internal integrity, and then it hurts. The feeling of discomfort will let you know. It says, "Sweetheart, take a look, get honest."

If you really believe in your product and in yourself, there is no selling, ever. When you think you know what's best for us, you hurt. The reality is that you don't know what's best for us. I don't think for a moment that I have something you need. If I believe that, I am insane. What I want for you is what you want for yourself. The only valuable skill is getting real.

If your mind is clear, you could walk out the door right now, with no friends, no job, no family, no money, no anything, and live absolutely happily. You can't *not* have abundance in paradise. In the stillness beyond belief, everything is known: where to go, what to do, when. All of it. The way I live is that I don't ever have to know anything again— not ever.

There is no way you can't have the best business on this planet. No one stops you but you—that's the only possibility. Your employees are not responsible for your success;

you are. And for those of you who are
employees, it doesn't matter who you work for,
if you do this Work, there is no way you can't
be a success.

When you've become a total success in
business and have more money than you
could ever spend, what are you going to
have? Happiness? Isn't that why you want the
money? Let's take a shortcut that can last a
lifetime. Answer this question: Who would
you be without the story "My future depends

on making a lot of money"? Happier. More relaxed. With or without the money. You'd have everything you wanted money for in the first place.

That belief that you need money keeps you safe, you think. "If I dropped the belief, who would be there to scare me into making money?" You use the belief that you need money, because you think that without it there would be no motivation. Can you know that? Can you know that if you didn't try to scare yourself into making money, you wouldn't have any, you would just sit there like a non-productive lump? And how do you react when you believe the thought that you would have no inspiration to make money? I've heard of incentives, but people take this a bit far.

It's good that you think you're going to lose your job. This is exciting. Do The Work, live The Work, notice, and know that if you lose your job, there is something better waiting for you. But when you're stuck in a belief, you're blind. There has to be something better, because there is only goodness in the universe. "Your life will be much better if you don't lose your job"—can you absolutely know that that's true? And there's nothing more exciting than living on the edge, and watching it.

My son lost a really big record contract, and he called me and said, "Mom, I am so excited. I lost a wonderful contract, and I'm so excited to see what's going to come that is better than that!"

I love it that the stock market is not going to cooperate in giving you a million dollars, if that's what it takes to bring peace and true happiness into your life. That's what everything is for. It leaves you to your own solution. So when you get all this money, and you're happy, totally happy, what are you going to do? You're going to sit, stand, or lie horizontal. That's about it. And you're going to witness the internal story you're telling now if you haven't taken care of it in the way that it deserves, and that is to meet it with understanding, the way a loving mother would meet her child.

If I had a lot of money, and someone told me
you were my friend because of that, I would say,
"Good." I don't care why—your motives are
not my business, you're my friend. Only *my*
motives are my business, and thank you for
being my friend. It doesn't matter why you're
my friend, the fact is that you're there for me,
you care about me, and the reason is not my
business. If you ask me for something and it's
honest for me to give it, I will, and if it isn't
honest for me, I won't. To think that you're
motivated by my money is to separate from
you. And if I'm not honest with my no's and
yeses, it could be that I am trying to buy your

friendship with my money. But when I'm clear, you are my friend again, inside me. I don't care what brings us together. If I think I know your motives, I have just cost myself a friend.

You can sit there and feel, "Oh, I need to do something with my stocks," and then you can inquire. "Is it true? I can't really know that." So you just let it have you. You just sit there with what your passion is, and read, and watch the internet, and let it educate you. And the decision will come from that, when it's time. It's a beautiful thing. You'll lose money because of that decision, or you'll make money. As it should be. But when you think you're supposed to do something with it and imagine that you're the doer, that's pure delusion. Just follow your passion. Do what you love. Inquire, and have a happy life while you're doing it.

The next time you give your children money, realize that the receiving is in the giving, that's it. If you touch it again, it's hot! The receiving is in the moment you give it. That's all you get. It's over. One thought about it after that is how you don't give the gift, it's a double loss. One expectation, one desire to have them be grateful, and you lose the gift. Love is an impulsive act, it's free. It's the story we tell about it afterward that's our poverty. My generosity is what's mine, the story you tell about it has no effect on me. What does that have to do with me? But my gift—that's what I receive. Attaching to these insane stories, without investigation, is how we cost us the gift that we are.

When you lose something, you've been spared—either that, or God is a sadist. How do I know I don't need the money? It's gone! I've been spared: what I would have done with that money would obviously have been much less useful for me than losing it.

Can you find one valid reason to keep the story that your husband shouldn't make a mistake with his business? I can't find one that doesn't hurt. Who would you be without the story? He might come in and say, "Oh my God, I made a huge mistake, I lost all our money," and you could say, "I understand that, we all make mistakes. What do you suggest? I'm here for you." And that's what we ultimately do anyway. On the other side of all the terror and blame, we say, "I love you. How can I help?" That's who we are. So what The Work does is cut to the chase. Who would you be without the story that he shouldn't make a mistake? He'd have a home to come to, and you would be that home, and you would have a home to go to in him, which is a comfortable place.

Doing The Work on job-related issues can have far-reaching consequences. When I work with corporations, I sometimes invite all the employees to judge each other. This is what employees and bosses have always wanted: to know how they look from each other's point of view. And then, after the judgments, they all do The Work and turn it around. The result can be a startling increase in clarity, honesty, and responsibility, and this, in turn, inevitably leads to a happier, more productive, and more efficient work force.

If I hire you and you don't meet the requirements, I thank you for all that you offer, and I fire you. Maybe I talk with you first, to see if there's something about your job performance that I may have missed. And if you don't meet my requirements, I thank you, because I know you've done the best you could, and I fire you, and I hire someone who's qualified to do what I want. It's not up to my employees to accomplish what I want, it's up to me; I'm the boss. And the reason that firing you is so kind is that I have just released you from a torture chamber, and allowed you to move into a space where you *are* qualified.

And because of my clarity and kindness, the space is open for the right person to move into it. Anything less than that is masochism: it's unkind to you and to me.

The reason I love this Work is that we begin now. It's much more fun than running a business; you are running something much more important. And your company will follow, because when the boss is clear, the employees become clear. The more clarity you live within your company, the more you get.

Your employees have to be attracted by that, even if they're not aware of it. There's nothing more efficient than a boss in whose presence people can be themselves.

Whenever you think that your needs are not being met, you're telling the story of a future.

Financial security is only a state of mind. The worst that can happen is a belief about what losing all your money would be like. Close your eyes, get your shopping cart, find your city, you are out there on the streets, check out your environment, make friends with what you see, go into your worst nightmare on the streets. You're a bag lady. There's no way out. No one is coming to save you. It is your projection about how we are on the streets that scares you. When you get there—and I have been there—the worst that can ever happen turns out to be the sweetest thing. My first experience of freedom from this fantasy was when I was in a warm place having a cup of tea, and it was very cold outside, it had frozen and rained and snowed, and I was in this warm place. And I saw a homeless man who had obviously slept outside all night. He had just a thin blanket, and I couldn't imagine how he hadn't frozen to death. But sanity doesn't suffer. When the mind is clear, there is no time when we can't go to some warm place and get out of the cold. In this stillness, we know where to go and what to do. But with a confused mind, we can't see that, and we chase after money and we save it and we're miserly with it, so that this nightmare doesn't happen, and the nightmare itself is an illusion. This homeless man didn't have enough sense to come out of the cold, his mind wasn't clear enough. And here is how you stay cold: it's freezing outside, you have only a very light blanket, and you think, "I could go into this building but no, I look too shabby, they'll never let me in." Can you see how inquiry won't hold that? "They'll never let me in"—can I really know that? How do you react when you believe that they won't let you in? You freeze. "There's no place to go"—is that true? Who would you be without the thought? Clear enough to step in out of the cold, to know where to go and when. You are the worst that can happen, your thinking

is the worst that can happen, and you scare
yourself, so that you have to go out and get
money and be a miser. "I don't want to do
God's will and be a bag lady on the streets, I
am of much more value over here in my nice
warm home"—can you really know that?

You're the one calling the shots on what is a
mistake in your business and what isn't. In
reality there are no mistakes. There are no
accidents, but that's a bit advanced for some
of us.

Does the wind blow? Did you experience rain today? That's it: what is is. We make mistakes, we don't, the wind blows, it doesn't, it is what is. Your story about it—that's where the heaven or the hell is. But one thing you can count on is that people will make what you consider mistakes. You can fire them, you can yell at them, you can divorce them, and the person in front of you is going to make a mistake, count on it. So all you have got going is to sit and investigate that concept. That's as good as it gets. If you attach to "He shouldn't make a mistake," welcome to hell.

The story "I need more money" is what
keeps you from realizing your wealth. You're
supposed to have exactly as much money as
you have right now. This is not a theory, this
is reality. How much money do you have?
That's it. You're supposed to have exactly that
amount. If you don't believe it, look at your
checkbook. How do you know when you're
supposed to have more? When you do. How
do you know when you're supposed to have
less? When you do. This is true abundance.
It leaves you without a care in the world.

There is nothing that this Work can't blend with. I hear from CEOs, barbers, therapists, prison workers, doctors, who are finding that whatever else their jobs are, they are ways of giving people themselves back.

If I didn't have money, I would do whatever it took to pay my bills. I just wouldn't need a plan about how that was going to look. It would come to me to mop floors, to clean houses, and I'd love doing that. And one thing would lead to another, one job would

lead to another, I would do it all for my own
sake, and enjoy it all. I can't not be wealthy.
It has nothing to do with money.

You can take any job, any time, and except for
your belief systems, money is not a problem.
You can work in a hamburger joint and make
minimum wage. And you just hold to your
integrity, without any beliefs about how that
should look, and eventually you could own
the whole chain. Because we are attracted to
that kind of integrity, and money can't buy

it, so we will give you anything to be in your presence, because everything is in order, and it's priceless.

In this country we have bankruptcy. If I put myself in trouble, I get myself out of it. And if I file for bankruptcy, I eventually pay every debt I owe, because living this way offers me the freedom I'm looking for. I don't care if it's a dime a month. I act as an honorable person, not because I'm spiritual, but because it hurts if I don't. Simple.

Your job is to appreciate what is, and that includes appreciating your boss. To appreciate him is to appreciate yourself.

I never lend people money. I *give* them money, and they call it a loan. If they repay it, that's when I know it was a loan.

God's will for me is that I not own anything, however many possessions I apparently have.

So I love it when people come and steal all my things; that way, I can see if there's one little attachment left in me, one little place of entitlement. Because there is only one joy in life: undoing myself. That is total surrender, surrender of the beliefs that you think will keep you safe. You can't let go of your possessions, it doesn't work like that. You investigate your beliefs about father or mother, for example, and something happens that's totally unrelated, and you experience freedom. Thieves take everything you own and people are saying, "Oh, you poor thing, how terrible for you," and you don't feel terrible at all, you feel amused, you feel exhilarated, because you're awake to all the stressful thoughts that might arise. And you haven't done anything but let go of a belief.

I knew a woman who had megabucks. Her father adored her, she adored him, and giving her money was one way that he showed his love. It was an incredible gift, and the way that she took it from herself and lived in poverty was that she believed she didn't deserve it. She believed that you had to do something to deserve all that money. And she found out that that thought was a way of being separate from her father and from herself. There's a huge prejudice about people with money, and that's how we separate. She found out that she was just like her father, she was over-indulgent: she kept on giving her money to husbands who didn't earn anything after they married her. Her parents gave it to her, and she gave it to her husbands. It's called generosity, it's called love. And what she came to see was that she did it for her own sake, and to withhold it was where the pain was.

When I receive money, I am thrilled, just thrilled, because I'm fully aware that it's not mine, that I'm just a channel. I'm not even the caretaker. I get to be the observer of it. The moment I get it from over there, a need for it appears here. It's amazing.

How do you react when you believe the thought that if you had more money you'd be happier? You get not to be happy now. You get to put your whole life on hold until you have more money. It's so much easier to be happy now. And that happiness is what The Work brings you in every moment, until eventually the space gets so wide that it becomes very clear how to make money, it becomes clear that we have it, it becomes clear that there is nowhere to go, no one going, and that you are where you always wanted to be. This is it, this is what all your thinking has brought you to. And if you are here fully, *here* contains everything you ever wanted. It's very sweet, because *here* is where you always are.

Being present means living without control
and always having your needs met.

The whole world will tell you that you
shouldn't be messy. This is our religion.
But all the punishment in that concept, "I
shouldn't be messy," hasn't worked yet. A
messy mind is a messy life. It's hopeless to
try to clean up your house, your office, your
desk. But if you clean up your thinking, then
it's effortless for your office and your house
to be clean. You work with the mind, and your

life gets transformed. The mess in your office is not the problem. Your boss can say, "I'll give you a million dollars if you clean up your mess for one year," and that still won't work, because you don't know how. "I need to clean up my mess"? I need to clean up my thinking. There isn't anything else to clean up, and the rest will follow.

Abundance has nothing to do with money. Money is not your business; truth is your business. You're supposed to have more money than you have? I don't think so. You're supposed to have less money? I don't think so. You're supposed to have exactly what you have. If you don't believe it, look at your checkbook.

No one has ever had a money block, only a mental block.

Money is a wonderful metaphor. It flows from here to there, through all countries, through phone systems and wires. It shows us how to be, mentally: how to flow, how not have any barriers, how to take all forms. It shows how easy it is to come in and leave all the time. It's a great guru. If you did what money does, you would be completely in love with what is.

I am not going to get wealth on the other side of the truth; I am going to get something much more important than that, something so powerful that everything else looks like nothing. But as long as I think it should look like money, I am cheating myself.

In my experience, there's nothing more fun than self-realization. Isn't that why we want money—to bring us happiness and peace? And the beautiful thing about inquiry is you can do it from wherever you are—while you're making money, while you're at home, while you're with your lover, while you're with yourself. Life is internal.